St. Rose of Lima

ST. ROSE OF LIMA SCHOOL
RESOURCE CENTRE

The Wayland Library of Science and Technology

THE UNIVERSAL FORCES

PETER LAFFERTY

The Wayland Library of Science and Technology

The Nature of Matter
The Universal Forces
Stars and Galaxies
The Solar System
The Changing Landscape
Air and Oceans
Origins of Life
The Science of Life
Plants and Animals
Animal Behaviour
The Human Machine
Health and Medicine

The Environment
Feeding the World
Raw Materials
Manufacturing Industry
Energy Sources
The Power Generators
Transport
Space Travel
Communications
The Computer Age
Scientific Instruments
Towards Tomorrow

Advisory Series Editor
Robin Kerrod

Consultants
Professor D.C. Imrie, Dr B.R. Orton

Editor: Steve Luck
Designer: David West · Children's Book Design
Production: Steve Elliott
Art Director: John Ridgeway
Project Director: Lawrence Clarke

First published in 1990 by
Wayland (Publishers) Ltd
61 Western Road, Hove
East Sussex BN3 1JD, England

AN EQUINOX BOOK

Planned and produced by:
Equinox (Oxford) Limited
Musterlin House, Jordan Hill Road,
Oxford OX2 8DP

Copyright © Equinox (Oxford) Ltd 1990

All rights reserved. No part of this publication may be reproduced or utilized in any form or by any means, electronic or mechanical, including photocopying, recording, or by any information storage and retrieval system, without permission in writing from the publisher and copyright holder.

British Library Cataloguing in Publication Data
Lafferty, Peter
The Universal Forces
1. Physics
I. Title II. Kerrod, Robin
530

ISBN 1-85210-860-6

Media conversion and typesetting by Peter MacDonald, Una Macnamara and Vanessa Hersey
Origination by Hong Kong Reprohouse Co Ltd
Printed in Italy by Rotolito Lombarda S.p.A., Milan
Bound in France by AGM

Front cover: Patterns created when scratched metal foil is flattened between glass.
Back cover: A fluorescent tube.

Contents

INTRODUCTION   5

ELECTRICITY   6
Electric charges and fields • Static electricity •
Electrons on the move • Using electricity •
Semiconductors

MAGNETISM   16
Magnets • Magnetic field • Electricity and magnetism •
Electromagnetism • Generators and motors

LIGHT AND RADIATION   24
Reflection and refraction • Curved mirrors and lenses •
Waves of light • Colour • Lasers •
The electromagnetic spectrum

FORCES, ENERGY AND MOTION   36
Force and movement • Laws of motion •
Energy and work • Gravity

GLOSSARY   44

INDEX   46

FURTHER READING AND PICTURE CREDITS   48

Introduction

Electricity is the most useful form of energy there is. It holds the key to our modern civilization. More fundamentally, it also holds the key to the make-up of matter. The atoms of matter are made up of electrically charged particles, and are largely held together by electrical attraction. Electricity is thus a great universal force, dictating the nature of matter everywhere.

Closely linked to electricity is magnetism, another great force in the Universe. The two go hand in hand, considered within the science of electromagnetism. They also travel together through space as a wave motion, forming a family of electromagnetic waves. Most familiar are the waves by which we see – light.

Another great force acts throughout the whole Universe and in effect holds the Universe together. It is called gravity.

◄ Patterns created when scratched metal foil is flattened between glass. These patterns are called interference patterns because they occur when light waves interfere with each other.

Electricity

Spot facts

- About 3 million million million electrons pass through a burning light bulb every second.

- Electric eels store enough electricity in their tails to light up 12 light bulbs.

- A household light bulb would have to shine for 10,000 years to release the same amount of light energy as a flash of lightning.

- Electrons are not only particles, they are also waves! Electron waves are used instead of light waves in electron microscopes.

The world is built from atoms made from a small number of different particles. Most of the particles carry electric charges. It is the force between these charges that helps to hold atoms together. Taming the energy held in these charges – seen uncontrolled in a lightning flash – has been one of the most important successes of science. Electricity has become our obedient servant, lighting our cities, turning the wheels of industry and powering our household gadgets. New ways of controlling electricity, using materials called semiconductors, have made possible modern electronics, such as those used in radios, record players, televisions and computers.

▶ The bright lights of Los Angeles. Electricity is the servant and messenger of the modern world. It is the most convenient source of power ever discovered. It supplies light and heat as well as mechanical power. It is also easily and cheaply carried along wires or cables.

Electric charges and fields

The origin of electricity lies inside the atoms that make up matter. Electrons and protons carry tiny amounts of electricity. They are said to have an electric "charge". There are two kinds of electric charge. The electron has one kind, called a negative charge. Protons have the other kind, called a positive charge. If two negative charges or two positive charges are brought close together, they repel each other and push apart. If a positive charge is brought near a negative charge, the charges attract each other and pull together. In other words, like charges repel each other, and unlike charges attract each other.

Normal atoms have no overall electric charge. The same number of negatively charged electrons orbit the nucleus as there are positively charged protons in it: the negative and positive charges are balanced. However, atoms and the objects that they make up can become electrically charged by losing or gaining electrons. If an object gains electrons, it becomes negatively charged. If the object loses electrons, it becomes positively charged.

Electric fields

The region around a charged object or particle, where the electric force can be determined, is called an electric field. The strength of the field at a particular point depends on the size of the charge on the object and the distance between the point and the object. The field becomes stronger the closer the point is to the object.

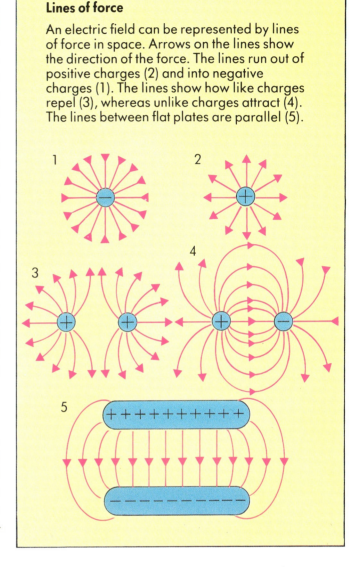

Lines of force

An electric field can be represented by lines of force in space. Arrows on the lines show the direction of the force. The lines run out of positive charges (2) and into negative charges (1). The lines show how like charges repel (3), whereas unlike charges attract (4). The lines between flat plates are parallel (5).

◂ Here, particles with opposite charges move in a bubble chamber. A magnetic field makes the particle tracks spiral in different directions. The green tracks are made by electrons with a negative charge. The red tracks are made by positrons, particles with the same mass as electrons but carrying a positive charge. Electrons are normally found orbiting the central nucleus of an atom. Electrons are also the origin of electricity.

Static electricity

If you rub a balloon on a woollen sweater, you give the balloon an electric charge. The rubbing transfers electrons from the sweater on to the balloon. The balloon gets a negative electric charge because of its extra electrons. If you hold the balloon up to a wall, the balloon sticks to it. The negatively charged balloon is attracted to the positive charges in the wall. If you rub two balloons on wool and put the balloons next to each other, they push apart. This shows that similar charges repel each other.

In these experiments, you have been making and using static electricity – electricity that does not move but stays in one place. The ancient Greeks, about 2,500 years ago, did similar experiments by rubbing a piece of amber – a fossilized resin material – with fur. The word electricity comes from elektron, the Greek word for amber.

When you walk across some types of nylon carpet, static electricity builds up on you. If you touch something metallic, small sparks will jump from you to the metal. When you take off a nylon shirt or blouse, you can sometimes hear a crackling sound, and see small sparks. These sparks are like miniature lightning flashes.

Lightning conductor

In 1752 a famous American scientist and inventor called Benjamin Franklin did a dangerous experiment. He flew a kite during a lightning storm. Electricity flowed down the string of the kite, making a small spark on a metal key near his hand. This showed that lightning was just a large electric spark. Later, Franklin used his discovery to invent the lightning conductor. This is a metal strip that runs from the top of a tall building to the ground. It carries the electricity safely away if lightning strikes the building.

▶ Lightning is caused when a large electric charge builds up on a cloud as the result of ice and water particles in the cloud rubbing together. Positive charges build up at the top of the cloud and negative electrons at the bottom. The electrons suddenly leap from the cloud to the ground, or to another cloud.

▲ An electronic flashgun uses devices called capacitors to store electric charges. Capacitors are also used in computer memories and radio circuits.

◀ This child's hair is standing on end because it is electrically charged. Some electrons have rubbed off her hair on to the comb, giving her hair a positive charge. Because each of her hairs has the same charge, they repel each other and stick out.

Electrons on the move

A simple electrical circuit

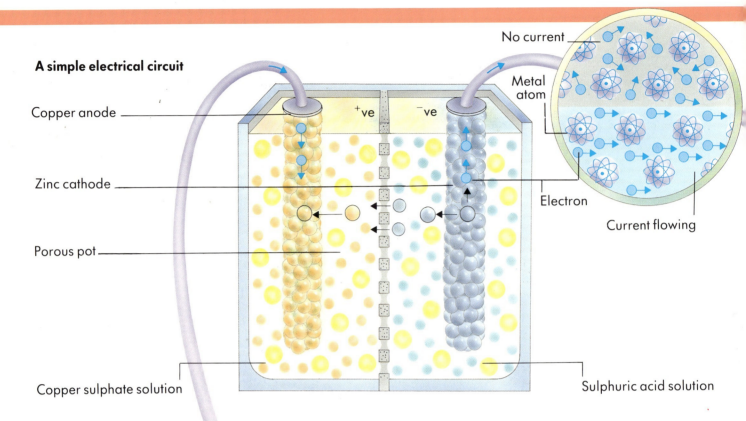

▲ A simple type of cell, or battery, called the Daniell cell. It contains a copper anode (positively charged electrode) in a copper sulphate solution and a zinc cathode (negatively charged electrode) in sulphuric acid. Atoms in the zinc cathode give up electrons, which flow through the circuit and form the current. When the electrons reach the anode, they combine with copper ions from the solution to form atoms of copper. The result is a flow of electrons from cathode to anode.

When a wire is connected to a battery in a continuous path or circuit, the electrons in the wire move along it. An electric current flows through the wire like water flowing through a pipe. But to make water flow through a pipe, a pump is needed to produce a pressure difference between its ends.

In an electrical circuit, the battery acts like an electron pump and produces an electrical pressure difference. The electrical pressure supplied by the battery is called the potential difference. It is measured in units called volts, which are named after the Italian scientist Alessandro Volta, who invented the electric battery in 1800.

The greater the voltage, the more electrons flow in the wire. We could try to measure the amount of current by counting the number of electrons that pass by. But this would be impossible because there are huge numbers of electrons in most electric currents. Instead, scientists measure electric current in amperes. One ampere is equal to a flow of about 6 million million million electrons every second. The ampere is named after a French professor of mathematics, André Marie Ampère, who did important work on the magnetic effects of electric currents in the early 1820s.

▼ An ordinary but dangerous light bulb (here shown broken but still working) glows as the electric current flows through the filament. The thin filament has a high resistance and is made from tungsten.

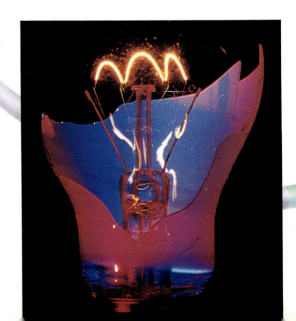

◀ In a metal wire, electrons are free to move about in any direction. As soon as a voltage is applied, as in a circuit containing a battery, the electrons move towards the positive terminal, or anode, of the battery.

▲ A space satellite, such as the *Hipparcos* star-mapping satellite shown here, uses solar cells to generate electricity from sunlight.

▼ Electrical resistance occurs when the flow of electrons is slowed down by collisions with the metal atoms or with impurity atoms in the metal. The electrons lose energy to the atoms. A component with a known resistance is called a resistor.

The dry battery

A dry cell, or battery, has a rod of carbon down its centre, acting as the anode, or positive terminal. The cathode, or negative terminal, is the zinc casing. Paper soaked with ammonium chloride solution lines the casing. A chemical reaction causes the zinc atoms to produce electrons, which are able to flow around a wire connected between the terminals. A black powder of manganese dioxide surrounds the carbon anode.

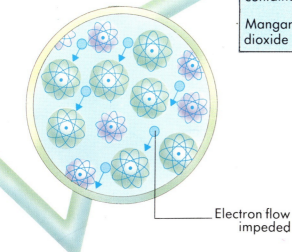

Electrons slow down as they travel through a wire, just as water slows down when it flows in a pipe. This slowing effect is called resistance. The more resistance a circuit has, the harder it is to keep the electric current flowing. A battery with a high pressure, or voltage, is needed to drive a current through a circuit with a large resistance. The amount of resistance in a circuit is measured in units called ohms, after the German scientist Georg Simon Ohm. In 1827 he discovered that the resistance of a wire is equal to the voltage divided by the current. This relationship is called Ohm's law.

Using electricity

When an electric current flows through a wire, the wire heats up. This is because of the resistance of the metal in the wire. The electrons jostle against the atoms of the metal, causing them to move. This raises the temperature of the wire because higher temperatures are linked to faster movements of atoms. The greater the resistance of the metal in the wire, the more energy the electrons lose to the atoms, and the greater is the heating effect of the electric current.

In an ordinary electric light bulb, the filament is made of thin wire, because the resistance of a thin wire is greater than that of a thick wire. The filament is also made in the form of a coil. This allows a greater length of wire to be used. A longer wire has greater resistance, and therefore gets hotter and brighter.

The heating effect of an electric current is used in a fuse. A fuse is a material of fixed low-resistance so that it stops conducting if an excessive current is passed through it. If a fault develops in an electrical circuit, too much electricity may flow along the wires and heat them up. Without a fuse this could start a fire.

▼ Many children's toys use simple electric motors powered by batteries. These convert electricity into mechanical energy for movement.

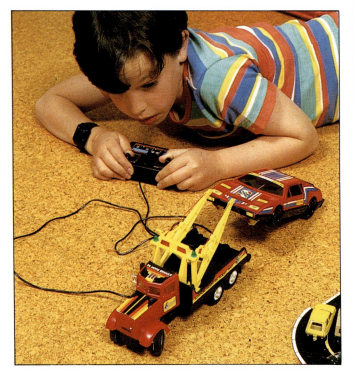

Bright lights

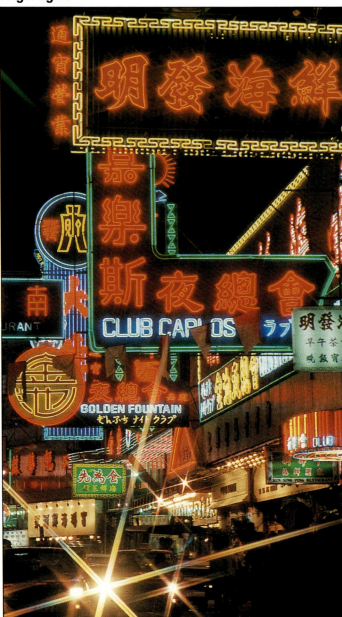

But if there is a fuse in the circuit, the fuse quickly melts. This breaks the circuit and stops the electricity flowing. The wiring cools down before a fire can start.

Electricity is especially useful and convenient because it can be made to do so many things. It can easily be converted into other forms of energy. A loudspeaker, for example, converts electricity into sound. Electricity can keep us cool when the weather is hot, and warm us

Coloured city lights are made from long, thin tubes that glow when electricity passes through them. They are called discharge tubes. A discharge tube is filled with a vapour or gas, such as neon, at very low pressure. When the tube is switched on, electrons are emitted by electrodes at the ends of the tubes. The electrons travel along the tube, striking the atoms of the gas and causing them to emit light. The colour of the light depends on the gas in the tube. Neon tubes glow bright red; argon tubes glow blue.

Fluorescent tubes are a type of discharge tube. The tube contains mercury vapour, which produces invisible ultraviolet rays when electricity flows through it. The rays fall on a fluorescent coating on the inside of the tube. This material absorbs the ultraviolet rays and re-emits them as white light.

Discharge tube

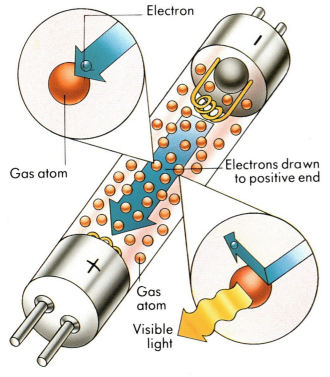

▼ Electroplating is used to coat a metal object with a thin layer of another metal. The object is hung in a tank holding a solution of the salt of the metal with which it is to be coated. A sheet of a metal is also hung in the tank. The object is connected to the cathode (negative terminal) of a battery, and the metal sheet is connected to the anode (positive terminal). The metal at the anode slowly dissolves, and the object becomes coated with the metal. All sorts of objects are electroplated, from silver teapots to chromium car bumpers.

Electroplating

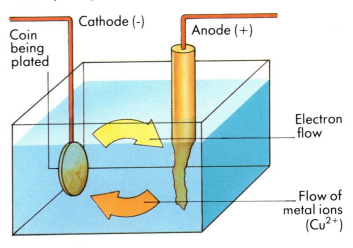

when it is cold. Electricity is vital to everyday life. Hospitals, schools, offices and shops would come to a standstill if it were not for electricity.

Electricity can be used to break a substance down into other substances. This process is called electrolysis. Electrolysis is used in industry to extract metal from mineral ores. For example, aluminium is prepared by passing an electric current through molten aluminium oxide, prepared from the mineral bauxite.

The current is passed via electrodes through a liquid called an electrolyte. If a current is passed through a solution of common salt (sodium chloride), chlorine gas is produced at the positive electrode, or anode. Sodium is released at the negative cathode. But it immediately reacts with the water in the solution to form hydrogen gas and sodium hydroxide. Chlorine, hydrogen and sodium hydroxide are all valuable substances made in this way.

Semiconductors

Semiconductors are materials that conduct electricity only with difficulty, unless they have been treated in some way. The most important semiconductor is silicon. Silicon is a successful conductor of electricity after minute amounts of other materials are added to it. This process is called doping. Silicon doped by adding minute amounts of phosphorus is called n-type; silicon doped by adding boron is called p-type. The effect of adding phosphorus to silicon is to add extra electrons. The extra electrons carry electricity through the silicon.

Adding boron to silicon also allows electricity to flow, but in a different way. Boron atoms have one fewer electron than silicon atoms. So when boron is added to silicon, there are places in the silicon where electrons are missing. These places are called holes. They act like positive electric charges, and carry electricity through the silicon in the same way as electrons. However, because they have a positive charge, they move in the opposite direction to the negative electrons.

Electronics engineers control the electrical properties of a semiconductor by adding precise amounts of impurities. This enables them to produce "integrated circuits". These have all the parts of an electronic circuit on a tiny silicon chip. Without them miniature televisions and personal stereos could not exist.

Inside a semiconductor

(1) Free electrons are the most important carriers of electricity in an n-type semiconductor. There may be a few holes. In a p-type semiconductor, holes are the main carriers of electricity, with a few electrons present. (2) In an n-type semiconductor, electrons are attracted to the positive terminal of the battery. In p-type material, the holes are attracted to the negative terminal. (3) When a slice of n-type material is joined to a slice of p-type material, only a small current flows when the negative terminal of the battery is connected to the p-type material. (4) When the battery is reversed, a large current flows because both holes and electrons move freely. This set-up acts as a semiconductor diode, which allows current to flow in only one direction.

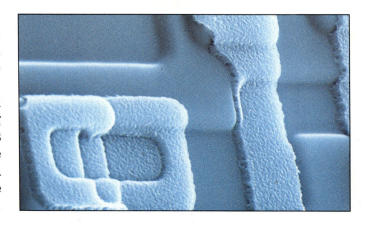

▲ A magnified view of a computer memory chip made of millions of "cells". Each cell can trap an electric charge representing a part of a number and hold it for reading.

◄ Removing silicon wafers from the doping oven. This is one of many stages in the production of silicon chips. During the doping operation a mask is applied over the wafer so that the dopants, such as boron and phosphorus, reach only certain areas.

► The chips on a wafer are tested and any faulty ones marked. The wafer is then cut into individual chips, and the faulty ones thrown away. The chips are put into a small plastic box, or case, with "legs", which act as connections to an external circuit. The circuits on the chip are connected to the legs by gold or aluminium wires.

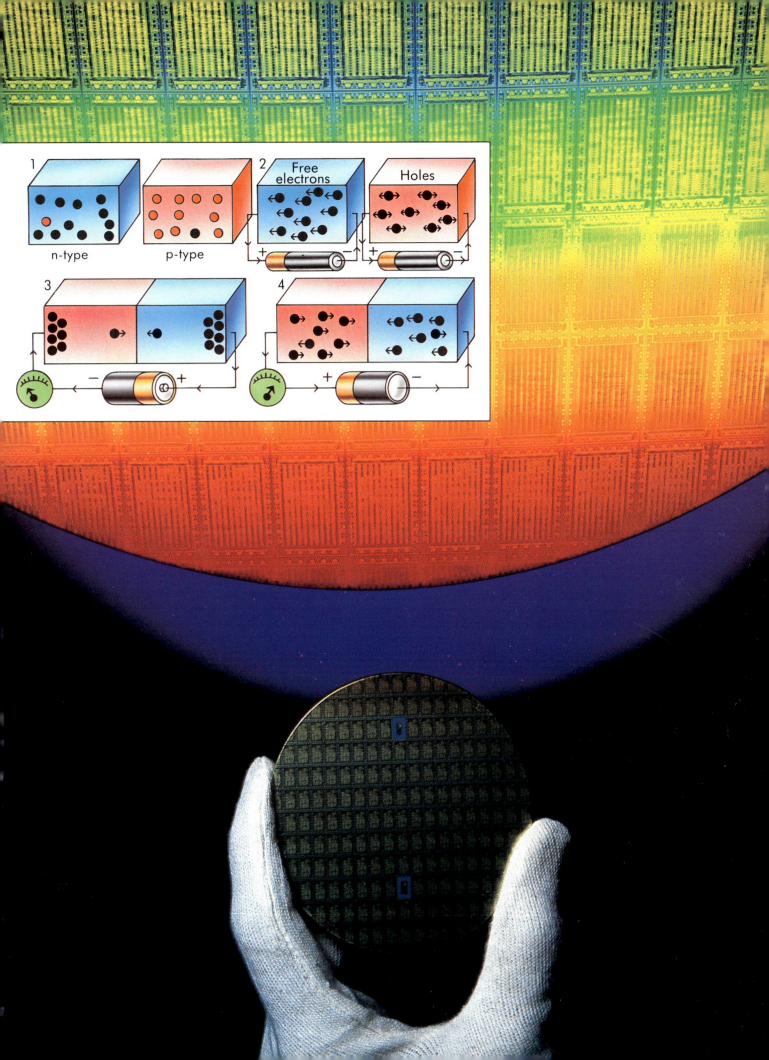

Magnetism

Spot facts

- A large electromagnet at the National Magnet Laboratory, USA, gets so hot that it needs 9,000 litres of cooling water every minute.

- The magnetic force around the giant planet Jupiter is 250,000 times greater than that of the Earth.

- The Earth's magnetic effects can be felt some 80,000 km out into space.

- The Earth's magnetism reverses its direction from time to time. The last reversal took place about 30,000 years ago.

- Migrating animals probably use the Earth's magnetism to help them find the way.

The ancient Greeks, more than 2,500 years ago, knew about magnets. They had discovered rocks which would attract small iron nails. Greek travellers told stories of mountains that could draw nails out of ships. These tales were untrue, of course, but they do demonstrate that at that time the Greeks knew about magnetism. It was not until the reign of Elizabeth I that the scientific study of magnets began. An English doctor, William Gilbert, pioneered the study of magnets and concluded that the Earth itself was a huge magnet. In 1820 the next advance was made by a Danish scientist, Hans Christian Oersted. He discovered that an electric current could produce magnetic effects. This form of magnetism, called electromagnetism, is used in electric motors and devices such as door bells and telephones.

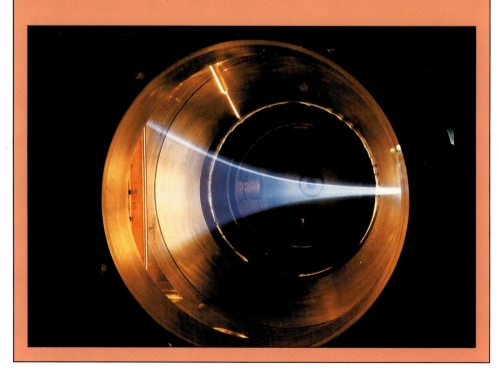

▶ A huge electromagnet shapes a blue haze of hot hydrogen inside a device which attempts to harness the power of nuclear fusion. This is the process which produces the Sun's energy. A strong magnetic field is used to contain the very hot material that is produced by the fusion process.

Magnets

Magnets attract things made of iron or steel. Some other metals, such as cobalt and nickel, are also attracted to a magnet. But most metals, such as gold, copper and aluminium, are not attracted in the same way. Neither are plastics, paper, cloth and glass attracted to magnets. These things are said to be non-magnetic.

Iron filings stick to a magnet most strongly at two points, usually near its ends. It is at these points, called the poles, that the magnet's power is strongest. One of them is called the north pole; the other is called the south pole. If a bar magnet is hung at its centre on a thread so that it can swing freely, the north pole points to the north. This effect is used in a compass. All planes and large ships are fitted with a compass as a vital part of the navigation system.

If you put the north pole of one magnet near the north pole of another, the magnets push apart, or repel each other. Two south poles behave in the same way and also repel each other. Magnets attract each other only if different poles are close together. Scientists say: "Like poles repel, unlike poles attract".

A giant magnet

The Earth acts as if it were a giant bar magnet, and has two magnetic poles. The Earth's north magnetic pole is in the Canadian Arctic, about 1,600 km from the true, or geographic, North Pole. The south magnetic pole is in Adélie Land about 2,400 km from the geographic South Pole in central Antarctica. The magnetism of these poles makes the north pole of a compass needle point to the north, and the south pole of a compass point south.

But because the Earth's magnetic and geographical poles are in slightly different locations, a compass does not point exactly due north or south. The slight difference between the magnetic and geographical poles is called the magnetic variation. It changes all the time. Navigators and mapreaders must allow for it when finding their way.

The Earth's magnetism is produced by the molten metal deep within the Earth's core. As the Earth spins, electric currents are created in the molten metal. These currents produce the Earth's magnetic force.

Earth's magnetism

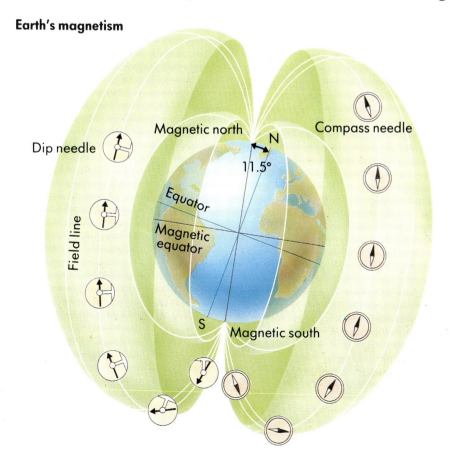

▲ Iron filings cluster around the poles of a magnet, where the magnetic force is strongest.

◀ We live on a huge magnet! Magnetized needles that are free to rotate point more or less towards the Earth's magnetic poles.

Magnetic field

The space around a magnet, where the magnetic force can be detected, is called a magnetic field. A kind of map of a magnetic field can be made with iron filings. Put a magnet under a piece of white paper and sprinkle iron filings on top. Tap the paper gently. You will see the filings form a pattern of lines. These lines follow the lines of force of the magnet.

The lines of force are close together near the poles, where the effect of the magnet is concentrated. Away from the poles, the magnetic effect is weaker and the lines of force are farther apart. The lines show the force a small north pole would experience in the field.

How are magnets made? One way is by stroking a piece of steel, such as a thin needle, with a magnet. To understand why this happens remember that the needle, like all other things, is made up of atoms. In a magnetic material, such as iron or steel, the atoms are like miniature magnets.

The atomic magnets are grouped together into small areas called domains, which are like mini-magnets inside the material. When an iron needle is stroked with a magnet, the domains become lined up so that they all point in the same direction. In this way the needle has become magnetized.

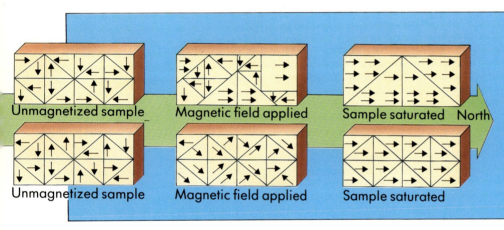

Magnetic domains

In a magnetic material, the atomic magnets form small regions called domains. In an unmagnetized sample, the domains usually point in different directions, producing no magnetic effect. When a magnetic field is applied (top), domains that are aligned with the field grow, and the material becomes magnetized. In strong fields (below) the domains rotate to become aligned.

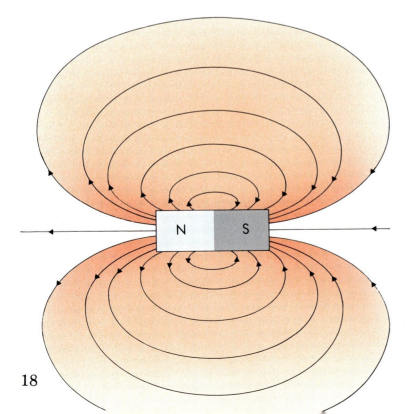

◄▼ A magnetic field can be represented by lines, called lines of force, linking north and south poles. The arrows give the direction of the force on an imaginary north pole. Similar magnetic poles repel each other, giving a "neutral point" between them where there is no force. Unlike poles, on the other hand, are attracted to each other, with lines of force filling the space between them.

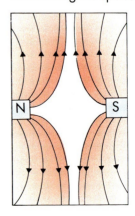 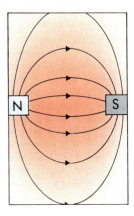

Electricity and magnetism

Moving electric charges – an electric current – causes magnetism. Indeed, magnetic fields are not truly different from electric fields. Rather, both are aspects of the same thing, the "electromagnetic field".

In 1820 the Danish physicist Hans Christian Oersted noticed that a current flowing in a wire deflected a compass needle nearby. It did not take long to discover that the magnetic field around a wire carrying a current is complicated. The strength of the field depends on several things — the strength of the current, the length of the wire and the distance to the wire.

In some instances, the field has a relatively simple form. Around a straight wire, the lines of force are circles. Around a solenoid – a coil with many turns – the field resembles that of a bar magnet. It has a north pole at one end and a south pole at the other.

Electromagnetic door bell

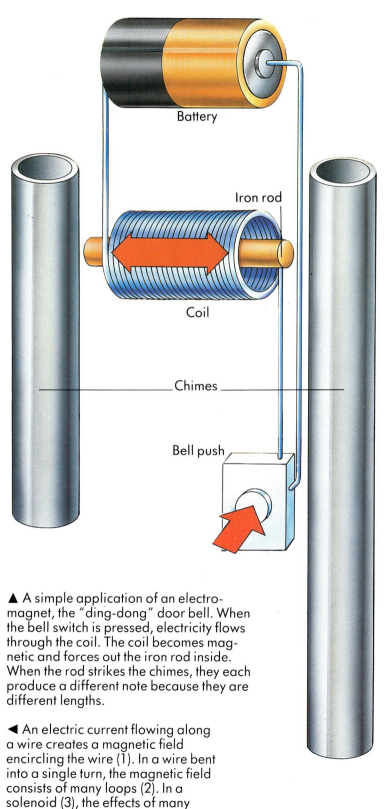

▲ A simple application of an electromagnet, the "ding-dong" door bell. When the bell switch is pressed, electricity flows through the coil. The coil becomes magnetic and forces out the iron rod inside. When the rod strikes the chimes, they each produce a different note because they are different lengths.

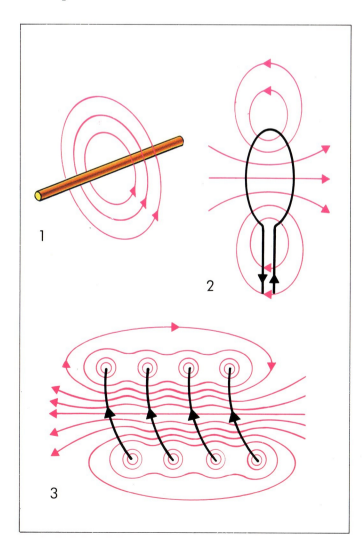

◀ An electric current flowing along a wire creates a magnetic field encircling the wire (1). In a wire bent into a single turn, the magnetic field consists of many loops (2). In a solenoid (3), the effects of many turns of wire add together to give a field like that of a bar magnet.

Electromagnetism

The first electromagnet was made in 1823 by an Englishman, William Sturgeon. He wound an insulated copper wire into a coil around an iron bar. When a current flowed through the coil, the bar became a strong magnet. The strength of an electromagnet depends on the number of turns of wire in the coil and on the strength of the current flowing through it. The more turns and the larger the current, the stronger the electromagnet becomes.

Super electromagnets
Today, the strongest electromagnets are made using superconducting coils. The coils are made of materials that lose all electrical resistance when they are cooled to very low temperatures, around −269°C. They can carry the large electric currents needed in powerful electromagnets. Superconducting magnets are used in particle accelerators, which are used for atom-smashing experiments.

Superconducting magnets are also used in medicine. They are an essential part of a type of body scanner, called a NMR scanner. These scanners use a process called nuclear magnetic resonance (NMR) to produce detailed pictures of the inside of a patient's body.

The patient lies in a strong magnetic field produced by an electric current flowing in a superconducting coil. Radio signals are beamed into the area of the body being investigated. The nuclei of the atoms of the body produce tiny magnetic signals, which are picked up by detectors. A computer is used to form a picture of the inside of the body from these magnetic signals.

Electromagnets are found in many household appliances. In a television set, electromagnets are used to control the beams of electrons that form the pictures on the screen. In a telephone, an electromagnet moves the plate in the earpiece that produces the sounds we hear. In a loudspeaker, electric currents produced by a record player or tape recorder are converted into sounds by an electromagnet. Electromagnets in the form of motors are also found in vacuum cleaners, food mixers, hair dryers and washing machines.

▶ A magnetic levitation train is held in the air by superconducting electromagnets. These magnets produce strong magnetic fields because large currents can flow through them without resistance.

▼ Very powerful electromagnets are often used in scrapyards. The magnetism does not exist when the current is switched off, and the magnet releases its load.

Moving-coil meter
- Scale
- Pointer
- Permanent magnet
- Spring
- Soft-iron core
- Coil
- Poles

▲ In a moving-coil meter a current passing through the spindle produces a magnetic field. This interacts with the permanent magnet, and the pointer records the current.

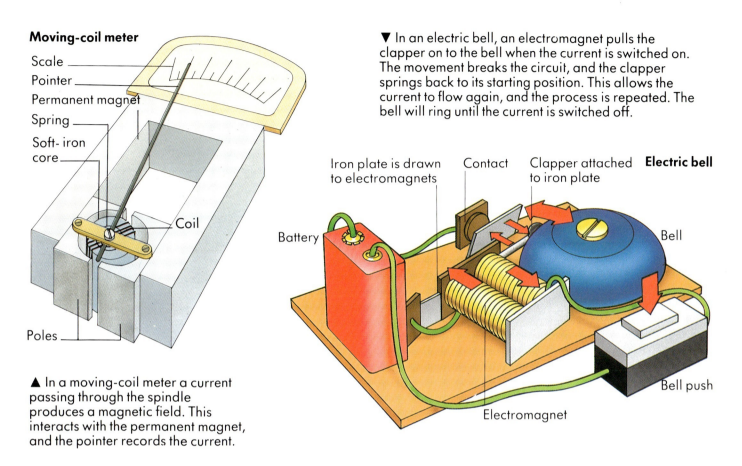

▼ In an electric bell, an electromagnet pulls the clapper on to the bell when the current is switched on. The movement breaks the circuit, and the clapper springs back to its starting position. This allows the current to flow again, and the process is repeated. The bell will ring until the current is switched off.

Electric bell

Iron plate is drawn to electromagnets · Contact · Clapper attached to iron plate · Battery · Bell · Electromagnet · Bell push

▼ Circuit-breakers are switches used in power stations. The magnetic effect of an excess current opens the switch, preventing the circuit becoming overloaded.

▶ A transformer consists essentially of two electromagnets. By altering the number of turns in the coils, it can be used to increase or decrease the input voltage.

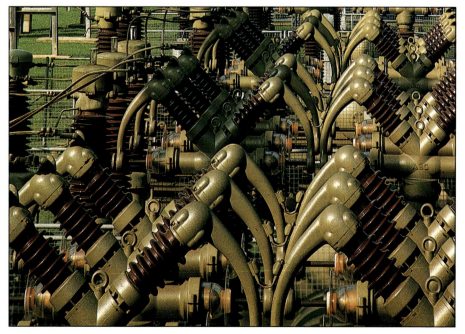

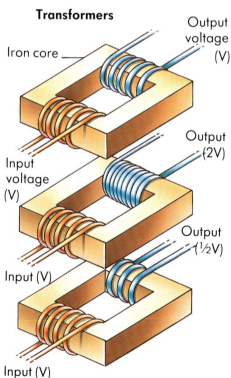

Transformers

- Iron core
- Output voltage (V)
- Input voltage (V)
- Output (2V)
- Output (½V)
- Input (V)
- Input (V)

21

Generators and motors

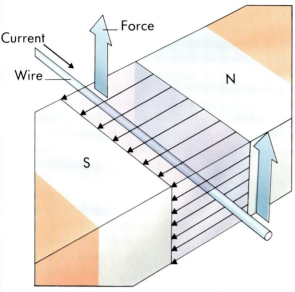

Principle of the generator and motor

When a wire moves in a magnetic field, a current flows if the wire is part of a circuit, because the electrons in the wire experience a force. This is the principle that underlies the operation of a generator. When a current flows in a wire in a magnetic field, the wire experiences a force. This is how a motor works.

Electrical generators and motors are related in the way they work. A generator converts energy of movement into electrical energy. An electric motor does the opposite; it converts electrical energy into energy of movement. The common factor between the two pieces of equipment is the effect of a magnetic field on moving electrons.

The electrons in a wire moving through a magnetic field experience a force, which sets the electrons moving along the wire. This is how a generator works. If the wire is in the form of a loop being spun in the magnetic field, the current produced moves first in one direction and then in the opposite direction. It happens because the two sides of the coil move alternately up and down through the field. This sort of current, which moves back and forth, is called alternating current (AC). It is the kind of electric current supplied by the electricity mains found in our homes.

It is possible to produce one-way electric current, or direct current (DC) from a rotating coil. A split ring, called a commutator, is attached to the ends of the coil. The commutator connects the coil to the circuit.

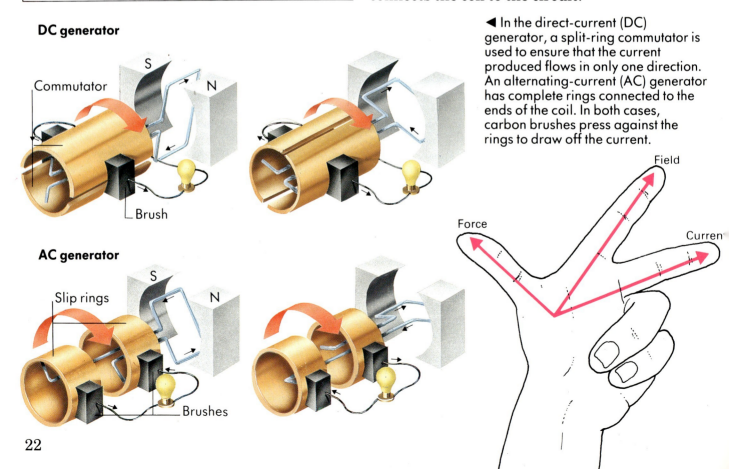

◀ In the direct-current (DC) generator, a split-ring commutator is used to ensure that the current produced flows in only one direction. An alternating-current (AC) generator has complete rings connected to the ends of the coil. In both cases, carbon brushes press against the rings to draw off the current.

In an electric motor, a current is set up through a wire placed in a magnetic field. The moving electrons then experience a force due to the magnetic field, which makes the wire move. If the wire is in the form of a loop, the forces acting on the two sides of the loop make it spin.

A simple motor requires an alternating current to make it work. As the coil turns, the current is reversed at the right moment to continue the rotation. In a direct-current motor, a commutator reverses the current through the coil at each half-rotation, and in this way keeps the rotation going.

There are various kinds of electric motors, used in factories, electric railways and household appliances. Most household appliances use a motor in which the magnetic field is produced by an electromagnet. The electromagnet is connected to the same electrical supply as the rotating coil. To increase the power, there are many coils in these motors. Each coil is in a slightly different position from its neighbours. The commutator is split into many segments, one for each coil. The motors are called universal motors, because they can run on both direct and alternating current.

▲ A powerful electric motor is used to drive a winch at a mine in Zimbabwe. The winch winds in a steel cable to raise a lift carrying rock from deep down the mine.

▼ Fleming's left- and right-hand rules. They indicate the directions of current flow, magnetic field and movement in motors and generators. The left-hand rule applies to motors, the right-hand rule to generators. The forefinger points in the direction of the field, the thumb of the motion, the middle finger of the current.

▼ In a direct-current motor, the commutator, which connects the coil to the current, reverses the direction of the electric current after the coil has turned half a turn. As a result, the coil keeps turning in the same direction. Without a commutator, the coil would come to rest after half a turn, with the coil horizontal.

▼ An alternating-current motor does not need a commutator because the current in the coil is continually reversing in direction. Instead it uses a pair of slip-rings, one connected to each end of the coil. The coil rotates at a speed which keeps it in step with the changes in the direction of the current.

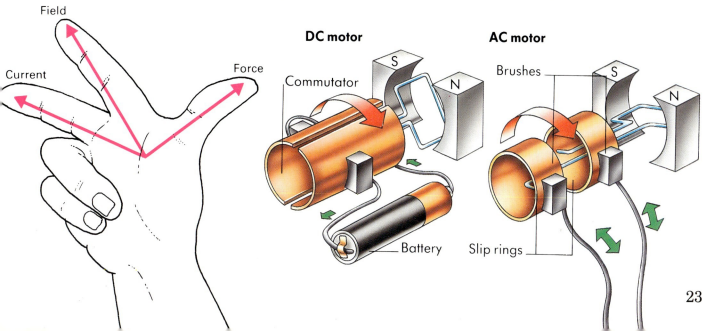

Light and radiation

Spot facts

• Light travels at a speed of 300,000 km/s. It takes one-tenth of a second to travel from New York to London, 8½ minutes to reach the Earth from the Sun, and 4⅓ years to reach Earth from the next nearest star.

• Albert Einstein, that most famous scientist, showed in 1905 that nothing could travel faster than the speed of light.

• Laser light beams shone from the Earth have been reflected off mirrors left by astronauts on the Moon. These experiments have been used to measure the precise distance to the Moon.

▶ A simple experiment that reveals much! When light passes through a prism, two phenomena occur. The beam bends away from its original direction. This bending is called refraction. The beam also disperses into a band of colours known as a spectrum. This shows that white light is a mixture of these colours.

Light shining through a hole forms a beam, or ray, that travels in a straight line. Light rays can be seen to bounce off mirrors, and bend when they enter a transparent material. But this is not the whole story. Light is also a form of wave, an electromagnetic wave. Furthermore, modern developments in the use of light, such as the laser, can be explained only if light also consists of packets of energy, or particles of light, called photons.

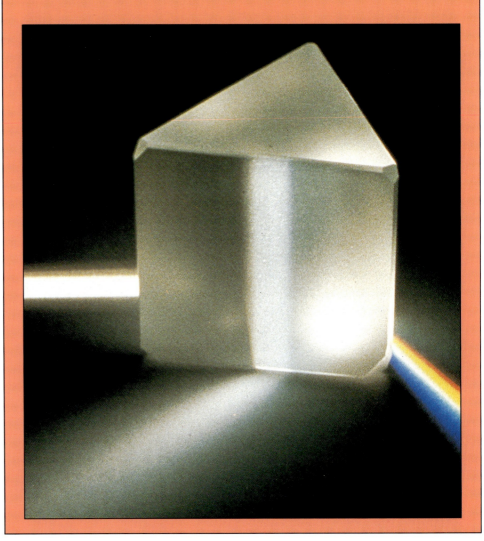

Reflection and refraction

One of the earliest discoveries about light was that it seems to travel in straight lines. Other discoveries concerned what happens to a light ray when it meets a surface, for example the surface of a mirror, or a glass surface.

When a beam of light falls on a shiny surface, it bounces off, or is reflected. The law of reflection states that the angle at which the ray strikes the surface, called the angle of incidence, is always equal to the angle at which the light beam leaves it. Simple diagrams using this law demonstrate how a mirror forms an image. The reflected image appears to come from behind the mirror.

Light rays bend when they enter a transparent material. This bending is called refraction. Refraction explains why it is so hard to spear a fish from the bank of a river. The fish is not where it seems to be, because the light from the fish is refracted as it leaves the water.

Refraction also explains why a drinking straw appears to be bent where it dips into a glass of water. Refraction occurs because light travels more slowly in water and glass, which are denser than air. This causes a light ray to swerve as it enters these materials, in the same way that a racing car swerves if it drives off the track on to a rougher surface.

◄ The John Hancock Tower in Boston, USA. The glass in many modern buildings acts like a giant mirror, often creating startling effects. The images in a mirror or reflected in a glass window are reversed left-to-right.

▼ The image of a tree reflected in a lake is upside-down and the same size as the real tree appears to be.

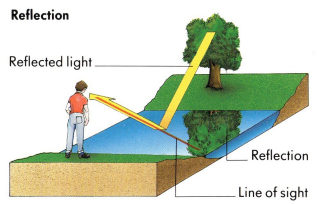

▼ A mirage of a tree in a desert is formed because light from a distant tree is refracted when it passes through the hot air near the ground.

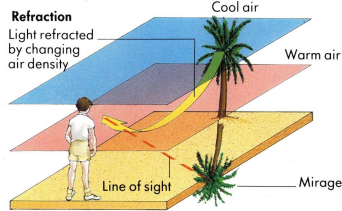

Curved mirrors and lenses

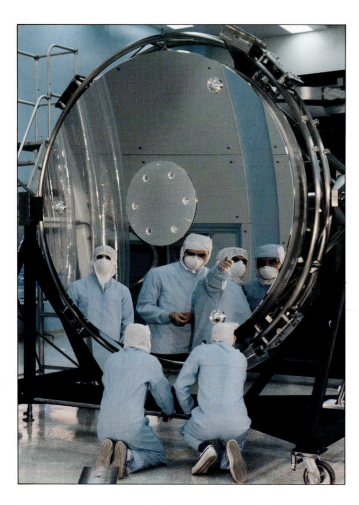

▲ Large astronomical telescopes generally use curved mirrors. This one is for the Hubble Space Telescope, to be launched into orbit on the Space Shuttle. Early telescopes used lenses, but produced poor images. Isaac Newton built the first reflecting telescope in 1671. Mirrors can be made much larger than lenses.

Mirror images

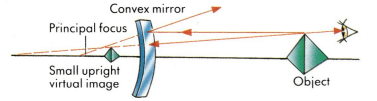

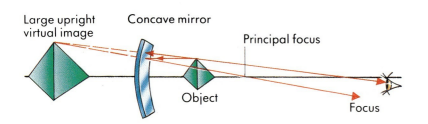

There are two kinds of curved mirrors: concave mirrors that bend inwards, and convex ones that bulge outwards. Concave mirrors are used in astronomical telescopes, shaving mirrors and in car headlamp reflectors. Convex mirrors are used for car rear-view mirrors and in supermarkets and shops to give the staff a good view of the shop floor.

If a beam of parallel light rays falls on a concave mirror, the rays are reflected so that they all pass through a single point in front of the mirror. This point is called the principal focus. Light falling on a convex mirror is spread out as if it were coming from behind the mirror.

Curved mirrors can produce images, or pictures, of objects placed in front of them. The size of the image and its position depends upon where the object is placed. If the object is far away from a concave mirror, no image can be seen in the mirror. However, if a piece of paper is held in front of the mirror, a small, upside-down image can be seen on the paper. This is called a real image. If an object is close to a concave mirror, a large upright image of it can be seen in the mirror. This kind of image, which can be seen in the mirror but not focused on to a piece of paper, is called a virtual image.

Lenses are pieces of glass or other transparent material with curved sides. They are used in cameras, small telescopes and spectacles. Convex lenses have sides that bulge outwards. Concave lenses have sides that bend inwards. Convex lenses can bring parallel light to a focus at one point, the principal focus. A concave lens makes parallel light diverge away from its focal point. Like mirrors, lenses can form images. The type and size of image depends on which type of lens is used and where the object is placed.

◀ A convex mirror produces a small, upright virtual image behind the mirror. A concave mirror produces a large upright, virtual image if the object is between the focus and the mirror. If the object is farther away, a small inverted (upside-down) real image is formed in front of the mirror.

▲ A magnifying glass is a convex lens. An object between the lens and its focus appears larger, or magnified, but can appear farther away from the lens than it really is.

◀ A lighthouse uses both mirrors and lenses to produce a powerful beam that can sweep the horizon. A solid lens would be too big and too heavy. Instead, Fresnel lenses, named after a French scientist, are used. In such a lens the surface is divided into a series of circles. Relatively thin ridges of glass are set in each circle at angles that would be found in a solid lens at that point.

Convex and concave lenses

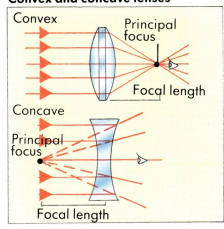

Convex lens image
Concave lens image

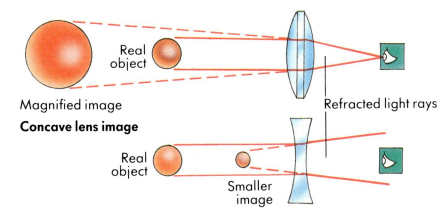

▲ A parallel beam of light entering a concave lens is bent to a single point known as the principal focus. On leaving a concave lens parallel light rays spread out as if from a point behind the lens.

▲ If an object is placed between a convex lens and its principal focus, an enlarged virtual image is seen through the lens. A concave, or diverging lens, always produces a smaller virtual image between the lens and the focus. A real image is one where the light rays actually come from the object. With a virtual image the rays only appear to come from the object and cannot be focused on to a screen.

Waves of light

What is light? Many scientists have studied light and tried to answer this question. In the late 17th century, the great English scientist Isaac Newton suggested that a light beam consisted of a stream of tiny particles, which he called corpuscles.

In about 1690 a Dutch physicist, Christiaan Huygens, put forward another idea. He thought that light travelled in waves. If you drop a pebble into water, you will see waves, or ripples move out from the point where the pebble hits the water. Huygens believed that light travelled in a similar way, but that the light waves were very small. He thought that the distance between the tops of any two neighbouring light waves was only a few ten-thousandths of a millimetre.

Although Huygens's theory explained the properties of light, such as reflection and refraction, it took many years for this theory to win support. In 1801 the Englishman Thomas Young performed an experiment which showed that light consisted of waves.

In Young's experiment, light from a small point source was shone on to a screen through two fine slits side by side. The light source was a sodium lamp, which gave light of a pure colour. Young saw a pattern of alternating light and dark bands on the screen. He realized that this result is similar to that seen when two stones are thrown into water at the same time. A series of waves is sent out by each stone, and where the waves meet, they combine. Where two wave peaks overlap, there is a peak of double height. Where two troughs overlap, there is a deep trough. This is called interference of waves. Interference could happen in Young's experiment only if light were a form of

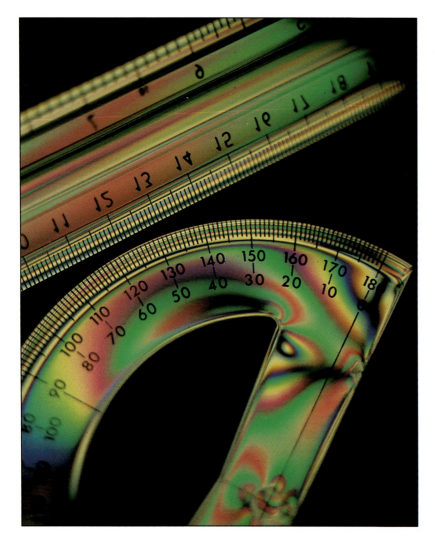

▲ Two stones dropped into a still pond produce circular patterns of spreading ripples. Where they meet, the two wave patterns interfere. Where the ripples cancel out, the result is still water. Where two crests combine, a large ripple results. Light behaves in the same way, but instead of ripples, light produces light and dark bands.

◀ Clear plastic rulers and protractors show coloured patterns in some lights. The colours are caused by the plastic splitting light into different beams, which then interfere with each other.

▶ Coloured patterns form in soap bubbles when light reflected from the top of the soap film interferes with light reflected from the bottom. The delicate, swirling rainbow colours seen in thin oil films on water are produced in the same way.

wave. With white light, Young's experiment produced a pattern of coloured bands. This is because the different colours that make up white light have different sized waves, which cancel out in different places.

The modern idea is that light waves consist of packets of light energy called photons. In some situations the photons are important, and light behaves like a stream of particles. In others the wave properties are more important, and light behaves like waves. So the two explanations by Newton and Huygens each provide a part of the answer to the question "What is light?"

▶ Interference patterns are produced when two beams of light, with their waves in step, overlap. Bright bands are seen where the waves reinforce each other. Dark bands are seen where the waves cancel out.

Colour

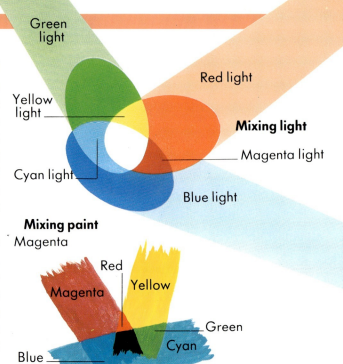

The colours of light correspond to waves of differing lengths. Red light, for example, has a wavelength – the distance between successive crests of a wave – of about 700 nanometres. One nanometre is equal to one thousand millionths of a metre. Violet light has the shortest wavelength in visible light. It is about 400 nanometres. Yellow, green and blue light have wavelengths between these values. White light is a mixture of light of all wavelengths.

When coloured lights are shone together onto a white surface, the colours are added together. Any colour can be produced by mixing combinations of red, green and blue light. These are the three primary colours of light and mixed in equal proportions produce white light. Two primaries, for example red and green, make a secondary colour, yellow.

Coloured objects or paints absorb, or subtract, certain colours from light and reflect the rest. Our eyes see the reflected light only, and so the object appears to be the colour of the reflected light. For example, red paint absorbs the green and blue colours in white light, and reflects only the red light. The secondary colours of light, yellow, magenta and cyan, are the primary colours of paint. Many colours can be made by mixing them; for example a mixture of magenta and yellow make red. All three mixed equally together make black.

▲ Mixing paints is different from mixing coloured lights, like those found in a theatre or disco. Many colours of paint can be produced by mixing magenta, yellow and cyan paints. With coloured lights, any colour can be produced by mixing red, green and blue lights.

▼ The lights of a disco help to enhance the music and create an exciting atmosphere. The lights are usually wired up to the loudspeakers so that they flash in time with the music. This is known as sound-to-light.

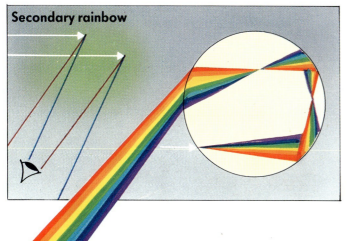

▲ The rainbow is a spectacular demonstration that shows white light to be a mixture of colours. Rainbows occur when sunlight from behind the observer is refracted and reflected by water droplets in the air. Often a fainter "secondary" rainbow is seen outside the bright "primary" one. The colours in the secondary bow are in the reverse order to those in the primary.

◀ In forming the primary rainbow, light from the Sun is first refracted as it enters a raindrop, then instantly reflected from the back of the drop. Finally it emerges, spread into a band of colours. In forming the secondary bow, the light is reflected twice within the raindrop before it emerges. In the primary rainbow the light is reflected only once.

Lasers

An American, Theodore H. Maiman, invented the laser in 1960. A laser is a device that produces a very powerful beam of light of a single colour. The word laser comes from a set of initials that stand for "light amplification by stimulated emission of radiation". This name was chosen because a laser persuades, or stimulates, its atoms to amplify, or make stronger, a flash of light.

Lasers are used in the home, factory, and hospital. A compact-disc player contains a low-power laser. The laser beam "reads" the music on the disc, just as the stylus reads the music on an ordinary disc. Low-power lasers are also used at supermarket checkouts to read the barcodes on packets of food. Surgeons use high-power lasers to carry out delicate eye operations. In industry, lasers are used to cut and weld metal sheets. When the Apollo astronauts were on the Moon, they set up a mirror pointing at the Earth. Later, scientists shone a laser at the mirror. By measuring how long it took the laser beam to travel to the Moon and back, the scientists were able to measure the distance to the Moon very accurately.

Lasers are used to create three-dimensional photographs called holograms. To produce a hologram, laser light is shone on the object being photographed. The light is reflected off the object on to a photographic plate. At the same time, some light from the laser is shone directly on to the photographic plate. The two beams of light produce a complex pattern on the plate. Later, if laser light is shone through the plate, a three-dimensional picture is formed.

▼ Lasers are key research tools. They provide a source of light of a single wavelength, or pure colour. Furthermore, the waves are all in step with each other. This greatly enhances the intensity of the light.

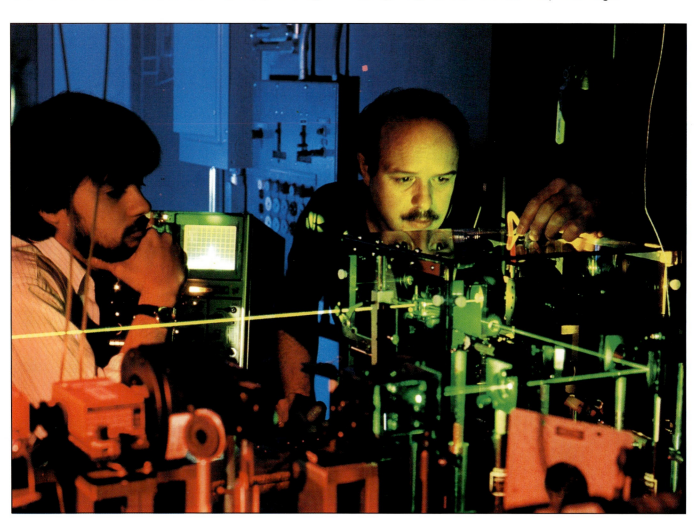

How a laser works

Electrons emit light when they lose energy. This happens when an electron jumps from one orbital to another one of less energy. As this happens, a photon is emitted.

When an electron in an atom is given extra energy, it is raised to a higher-energy orbital. The energized electron can then emit a photon and return to its usual orbital spontaneously. However, it can also be stimulated to fall back by a photon passing nearby. This is stimulated emission. The emitted photon and the passing photon move away in step, with their troughs and peaks matching exactly. The light produced in this way is said to be coherent.

The first lasers used a cylinder of ruby to produce their light. In the ruby laser a powerful flashlight tube is wrapped around the ruby cylinder. When the flash tube is turned on, the ruby becomes bathed in light. The ruby absorbs the light and its electrons move to high-energy orbitals.

One light photon is released, which then stimulates other energized electrons to release more photons. There is a rapid build-up of photons, until the light becomes bright enough to pass through a partly silvered mirror at one end. Ruby lasers are still used. Other types use gases or liquids.

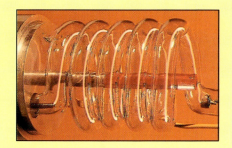

▲ The crystal and flashlight tube in a ruby laser. Crystals other than rubies have been developed for use in lasers. Most common are yttrium-aluminium-garnet (YAG) crystals, which allow the laser to operate continuously.

▼ When an atom absorbs light, electrons are raised to higher-energy orbitals. They can be stimulated to fall back to their usual orbital by a photon. When this happens, another photon is emitted, which moves away in step with the stimulating photon.

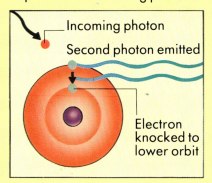

▲ Using a medical laser. Here a surgeon directs the beam from an argon laser through a small funnel into a patient's ear in order to remove a tumour between the ear and the brain.

Gas laser

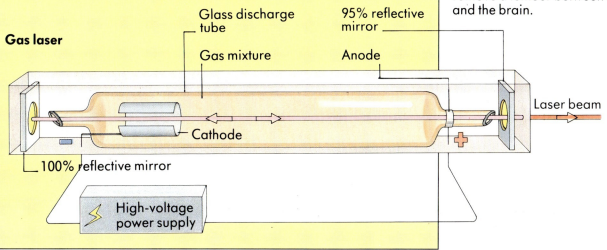

The electromagnetic spectrum

What bees see

The eyes of animals and insects are often sensitive to wavelengths we cannot see. The bee responds to ultraviolet light. A flower that looks a uniform colour to us, seems to have a dark centre to a bee, enabling it to find the pollen.

In 1865 the Scottish physicist James Clerk Maxwell used mathematics to show that waves which were a combination of electricity and magnetism, could spread through space. He called these waves electromagnetic waves.

You can visualize these waves by thinking about what happens when an electric charge is moved rapidly up and down. When still, the charge is surrounded by lines of electric force, which spread straight out from the charge. When the charge is moved up and down, the lines of force wiggle, in the same way that a stretched rope wiggles when one end is waved back and forth.

The wiggles in the lines of force move out from the charge in the same way that the wiggles move along the rope. However, the charge also generates a magnetic field as it moves, because it is a small electric current.

X-ray of a fractured leg

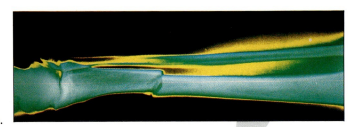

▼ The electromagnetic spectrum includes all forms of electromagnetic waves from gamma rays at the short-wavelength end to radio waves at the long-wavelength end. Visible light falls in about the middle of the spectrum.

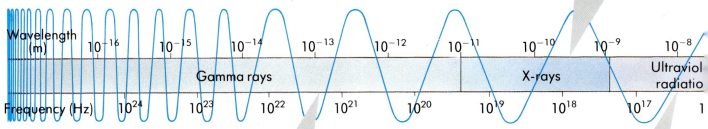

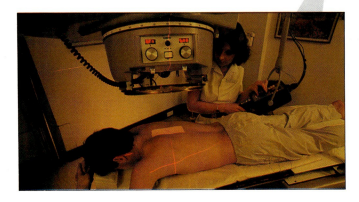

Gamma-ray therapy

An ultraviolet bed

The lines of magnetic force form circles around the moving charge. They move out from the charge like ripples moving across a pond. They move outwards at the same time and at the same speed as the electric wiggles. And so they form a wave that is a combination of changing electric and magnetic fields.

Maxwell calculated the speed of these electromagnetic waves to be the same as the speed of light, so he suggested that light consisted of electromagnetic waves. In 1889 the German physicist Heinrich Hertz produced radio waves and showed that they were electromagnetic waves too. They differed from light waves only in having longer wavelengths, or smaller frequencies. We now know that gamma rays, X-rays, microwaves, and infrared rays are all electromagnetic waves. They make up the electromagnetic spectrum.

Electromagnetic waves

James Clerk Maxwell described how electromagnetic waves consisted of electric and magnetic fields lying across the direction in which the wave is travelling. The electric field is at right-angles to the magnetic field.

Visible light fibre optics

A short-wave CB radio

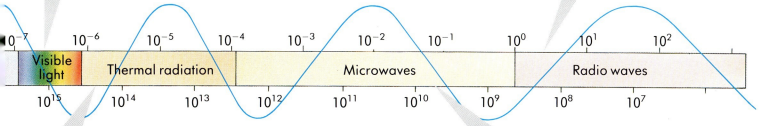

An infrared thermograph of a man smoking a pipe

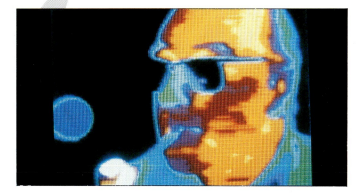

A microwave radar aerial

Forces, energy and motion

Spot facts

- On a 16th-century battleships, the guns were never fired at once. This would have created such a big reaction force that the ship would have overturned.

- A flash of lightning releases up to 3,000 million joules of energy. It needs 100,000 million joules to send a rocket into space. A tropical hurricane releases about 100,000 million million joules. Earthquakes can release up to 10 million million million joules.

- If you can jump 1 m high on Earth, you would be able to jump to a height of 6 m on the Moon.

▶ The Panavia Tornado fighter-bomber. As a jet aircraft moves through the air, it is acted on by a number of forces. The force of gravity pulls it down. However, its wings provide an upwards force, called lift, which keeps it in the air. The engines provide a forward force, which overcomes the resistance, or drag, of the air.

Imagine a ball being hit by a golf club. It is obvious that the force of the club on the ball starts the ball moving. But why does the ball continue to move after it has lost contact with the club?

The answer to this question can be found in the three laws of motion proposed by Isaac Newton in 1665. The three laws of motion explained how forces make objects move. These laws are still used today for tasks such as calculating the paths taken by spacecraft. Such calculations also make use of another great discovery by Newton: gravity. This is one of the great forces of the Universe, which attracts objects and makes them move.

Force and movement

Nothing starts moving by itself. A push or a pull is needed to start any object moving. These pushes or pulls are called forces. When you kick a ball, the force which starts the ball moving is provided by your foot. As well as starting things moving, forces can stop moving objects.

Friction

When a ball rolls across the ground, a force called friction acts on it, and eventually stops it moving. Without friction, the ball would go on moving at the same speed and in the same direction for ever. If a football bounces off a wall, the ball changes the direction in which it is moving because of the force exerted by the wall. Forces can speed up, slow down or change the direction of a moving object.

A seat on a fairground roundabout is continually changing its direction, so there must be a force acting on it. This force acts through the chain that holds the seat to the roundabout. If the chain were to break, this force would cease to act. The seat would fly off and continue in a straight line. Any force that produces circular motion is called a centripetal force. Centripetal forces act towards the centre of the circle.

Scientists believe that there are only four basic types of force. One is the electrical and magnetic force and another is gravity. The two other types of force, called the weak and the strong forces, are found only inside the atomic nucleus. All other forces are derived from these basic four.

▼ The people on a roundabout feel a centripetal force, acting towards the centre of their circular path. This force is a combination of their weight and the tension in the chain holding the chair. Confusingly, it is popularly called centrifugal force, which means one acting away from the centre.

Laws of motion

In 1687 the English scientist Isaac Newton set down three laws of motion, which show how forces affect moving bodies. The first law says that an object at rest will stay at rest unless a force acts on it, and an object moving at a constant speed in a straight line will continue at the same speed and in the same direction unless a force acts.

The second law says that when a force acts on an object, the object changes its speed or direction of motion in the same direction as the force that has been applied. The change of speed or direction is called the acceleration of the object. The greater the force acting on a body, the greater is the acceleration produced. The greater the mass of the body, the greater is the force required to move it or change its direction.

The third law says that for every force, there is an equal force acting in the opposite direction. Newton illustrated this law with the example of a horse pulling a stone tied by a rope. While a forwards force acts on the stone, the horse feels an equal force backwards.

◄ The launching of the Space Shuttle illustrates all of Newton's laws of motion. As predicted by the first law, before the motor fires, the Shuttle is still. In line with the second law, with the motors firing, the Shuttle lifts off the launch pad. The third law indicates that the upwards force on the Shuttle is equal and opposite to the force acting on the hot gases streaming from the engines.

▼ Some dragster engines deliver an enormous force, accelerating the car to speeds of over 400 km/h in as little as 6 seconds.

Using these laws, scientists are able to explain how objects move and what happens when they collide. The first law explains a simple party trick. If a tablecloth is pulled quickly and firmly enough, it can be taken off the table without disturbing the dishes on it. The point is that the dishes do not experience the force that pulls away the cloth, and so they stay undisturbed. Unfortunately, as many tricksters have discovered to their cost, there is another force which should be taken into account, friction. Friction is a force which acts when two surfaces rub together. It slows down the movement and may cause the dishes to move and crash to the floor.

One result of the second and third laws is that when objects collide, their total momentum does not change. The momentum of a moving object depends upon both the speed and the mass of the object. When a car is moving at a high speed, it has more momentum than when it is moving at a slower speed. Also, a heavy lorry has more momentum than a small car moving at the same speed.

Sometimes if a moving ball in a pool or snooker game collides with a similar but unmoving ball, the first one stops. The second ball moves off with the same speed that the first ball had before the collision. The momentum of the first ball has been completely transferred to the second ball. But the total momentum after the collision is the same as the momentum before the collision. When you jump up and down, you are like a small ball banging into a very large ball, the Earth. After the collision, you stop moving, and the Earth absorbs your momentum. You make the Earth move. But because the Earth is 100,000 million million million times heavier than you are, the movement is very tiny and you will not notice it.

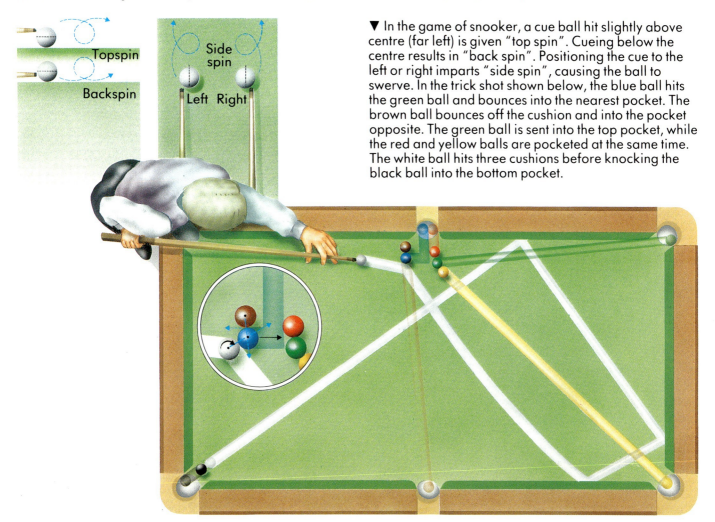

▼ In the game of snooker, a cue ball hit slightly above centre (far left) is given "top spin". Cueing below the centre results in "back spin". Positioning the cue to the left or right imparts "side spin", causing the ball to swerve. In the trick shot shown below, the blue ball hits the green ball and bounces into the nearest pocket. The brown ball bounces off the cushion and into the pocket opposite. The green ball is sent into the top pocket, while the red and yellow balls are pocketed at the same time. The white ball hits three cushions before knocking the black ball into the bottom pocket.

Energy and work

What is energy? We cannot touch it, see it, or weigh it. However, its effects are sometimes very obvious. When a lightning flash strikes, a bomb explodes, or a speeding train rushes by, it is clear that much energy is being used. The movement of the train shows one of the effects of energy. Nothing can move without energy. And because doing work involves movement, no work can be done without energy.

To a scientist, work is done whenever a force moves something. The greater the distance moved, and the greater the force involved, the more work is done. The more work done, the more energy is used. Work and energy are measured in units called joules, named after the British scientist James Prescott Joule, who lived in the 19th century. He did experiments to measure the heating effect of friction.

One joule is the work done when a force of one newton moves through a distance of one metre. A newton is a force that gives a mass of one kilogram the acceleration of one metre per second per second. This is equivalent to lifting a bag of sugar from one shelf to another in a cupboard.

It is clear that energy comes in different forms. Some forms of energy are obvious, others are more difficult to spot. A wound clock spring has energy because it can make the hands of the clock move. This form of energy is called stored or potential energy. Moving objects also have energy, called kinetic energy, because of their movement. Food contains energy in chemical form, which allows children to run about and play.

The different forms of energy can interchange. Electrical energy changes into heat energy in an electric fire. The chemical energy in food changes into energy of movement or heat in our bodies. The kinetic energy of the wind can be changed into electrical energy using a wind-driven generator. But when one form of energy changes into another, the total amount of energy remains the same. This is a statement of the law of conservation of energy.

▼ In 1977 a solar car drove more than 3,000 km across Australia in six days. The car had 7,200 solar cells arranged around its body, which converted energy in sunlight into electrical energy to power electric motors to drive the wheels. The top speed was 72 km/h.

Changing energy

(1) A hydroelectric power station taps the store of potential energy held in a water reservoir. As the water is released, its potential energy is converted into kinetic energy as it runs downhill. (2) Below the reservoir, the water drives round a turbine. (3) In the turbine, some energy is lost in doing work against friction as the turbine shafts rotate. This "lost" energy is converted to heat and sound. (4) The turbines drive generators, which convert the kinetic energy of the rotating shafts into electrical energy. (5) The electrical energy created by the generator is in the form of low-voltage alternating current. This is converted by transformers to high voltage for transmission. (6) Overhead transmission lines carry current at high voltage to reduce losses caused when electrical resistance creates heat. (7) Once the electricity reaches the consumer, it is converted to other forms of energy, such as light and heat. In the home, mechanical energy is produced in devices such as washing machines and lawnmowers.

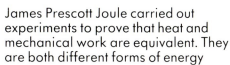

James Prescott Joule carried out experiments to prove that heat and mechanical work are equivalent. They are both different forms of energy

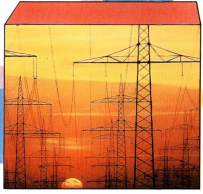

Gravity

The first person to realize why things fall to the ground was Isaac Newton. It is said that he was sitting in the orchard of his house at Woolsthorpe, in Lincolnshire, England, in 1665. He saw an apple fall from a tree. He realized that the Earth must be pulling, or attracting, the apple. He went on to discover that all objects attract each other. The attractive force between objects is called gravity. You can feel this force if you try to lift anything. The weight of an object is due to the force of gravity between the object and the Earth.

Newton realized that gravity was a long-range force. The force of gravity of the Earth reaches beyond the Moon. It stops the Moon from flying off into space. In turn, the Moon's gravity pulls the Earth's seas towards it, causing tides. The force of the Sun's gravity reaches far out into space and controls the movements of the planets.

Newton's studies of gravity revealed that the force of gravity gradually got weaker away from the Earth. Because of this, a person is attracted less in a high-flying aircraft than on the ground. However, the change in weight is very small and we do not notice it. At 25,000 km above the Earth, you would weigh only about one-tenth what you do on the ground.

The force of gravity is smaller on the Moon than on Earth. This is because the force of gravity depends upon the amount of matter in the objects being attracted together. The more matter, or mass, the objects have, the stronger the force of gravity between them. Because the Moon has only one-sixth the mass of the Earth, its gravity is only one-sixth that of the Earth. A person who weighs 60 kg on Earth would only weigh 10 kg on the Moon. Astronauts can throw things much farther and jump much higher on the Moon because of the weak gravity.

◀ An astronaut in orbit above the Earth appears to be floating motionless in space. But gravity has not ceased acting. He is falling freely and, at the same time, moving forward at great speed. The combination of the two movements produces a circular path that keeps him at the same distance above the Earth.

▼ According to modern ideas, the gravitational force of a large collection of stars, such as a galaxy, bends the space around it. This causes light rays to bend rather than follow a straight path. If a bright object, such as a quasar, is behind the galaxy, two slightly separated images of the quasar can be seen from Earth. One image is the direct view of the quasar; the other is due to the light bent around the galaxy. This effect is called a gravitational lens.

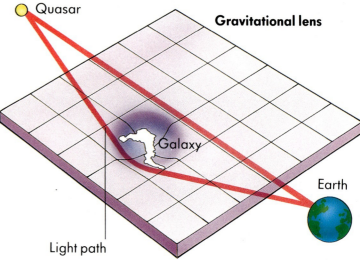

▲ Skydivers experience a force due to air resistance as they fall. This increases with speed, and at a certain speed becomes equal to the force of gravity, which is accelerating them downwards. When this happens, the divers fall at a constant speed, called the terminal velocity. Skydivers can reach a speed of 298 km/h in a head-first position in the lower atmosphere.

◀ The Italian scientist Galileo began the scientific study of moving objects in about 1590. He is said to have dropped objects of different weights from the Tower of Pisa, to show that all objects fall at the same rate. He also made many important astronomical discoveries using a telescope, which he constructed in 1609. He was the first to see the moons circling around the planet Jupiter.

◀ An experiment performed by Galileo involved rolling balls down a gently sloping plank and measuring the distance moved in equal intervals of time. Unfortunately, Galileo did not possess an accurate clock; he used a water clock. Nevertheless, he was able to show that the speed increased steadily as the ball moved down the slope. In other words, the force of gravity produced a steady acceleration on the ball.

Galileo's experiment

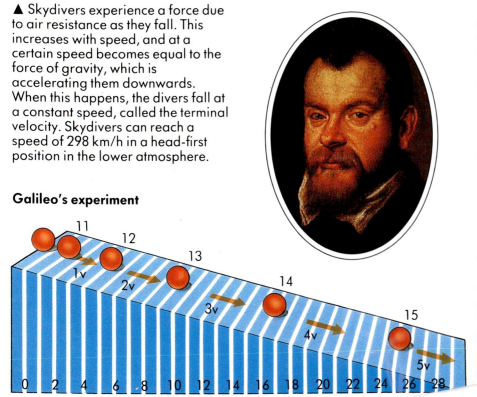

Glossary

AC Short for **alternating current**.

acceleration The rate at which the velocity of a moving body changes.

alternating current (AC) Electric current that travels first in one direction, then the other. Mains electricity is AC. It is produced by a generator called an alternator.

anode A positive electrode, for example, of an electric cell or electron tube.

battery A device for producing electric current by chemical action. The term is also sometimes used to refer to other devices for producing electricity, such as solar and nuclear batteries.

cathode A negative electrode, for example, in an electric cell or electron tube. In general it is a source of electrons.

cathode-ray tube An electron tube in which a beam of electrons is manipulated to form an image on a fluorescent screen. The picture tube in a TV set is a cathode-ray tube.

cell, electric A device that produces electricity. For example, a dry cell produces electricity by chemical means; a solar cell converts the energy in sunlight into electricity.

centre of gravity A point within a body or system at which the weight or mass of a body appears to be concentrated.

centripetal force A force on a body rotating in a circle, directed towards the centre of that circle, which keeps the body travelling in a circular motion.

circuit, electric The path along which electric current flows.

compass, magnetic An instrument for finding direction, which makes use of the Earth's magnetic field.

conduction The passing on, substance of electricity or heat (thermal conduction). In metals, which are good conductors, conduction is brought about by the flow of electrons.

current, electric The flow of electricty in a conductor, being the flow of electrons. By convention current is said to flow from the positive electrode to the negative. But the electrons in reality flow in the opposite direction.

DC Short for **direct current.**

diffraction The spreading out of a wave (water, light, sound) after it passes through a narrow aperture or round an obstacle.

direct current (DC) One-way electric current, like that produced by a battery.

electricity The effects brought about by the presence of positive and negative charged particles, and the flow of charged particles, usually electrons, through wires, gases and so on.

electrolysis Producing a chemical reaction in a substance in solution or when molten by passing an electric current through it.

electromagnet A temporary magnet consisting of a coil of wire wound around an iron core. It is a magnet only while electric current is being passed through the coil.

electromagnetic radiation A kind of radiation that consists of electric and magnetic vibrations, which travel in the form of a wave. It comprises a family of waves, which differ from one another in their frequency and wavelength. These waves include X-rays, light rays and radio wave.

electromagnetism The study of the close relationship between electricity and magnetism.

electron The smallest of the three main particles in atoms, which has a charge.

electroplating The coating of one metal on another by means of electrolysis.

elements, chemical Simple substances made up of atoms with the same atomic number. They are the building blocks of matter.

field The area in which a body exerts an influence, as in magnetic field.

force Commonly a push or a pull: something that, when it acts on a body, tends to change its state of motion or deform it.

frequency Of a wave motion, the number of complete waveforms (cycles) that pass a given point in a certain time. It is measured in hertz, or cycles per second.

friction A force that opposes motion between two surfaces in contact with each other.

gamma rays Electromagnetic radiation of short wavelength. Gamma rays are often given off in radioactive decay.

gas One of the three main states of matter, in which the particles travel freely at very high speed. Contrast **solid** and **liquid.**

Geiger counter An instrument for detecting and measuring atomic radiation.

generator, electric A device that produces electricity by converting mechanical energy into electrical energy. It uses the principles of electromagnetism.

gravity (or gravitation) The force of attraction that exists between any two lumps of matter. It is one of the basic forces of the Universe.

hologram A three-dimensional picture (that is, one with depth) created by means of laser light.

insulator A material that does not conduct electricity or heat well.

integrated circuit A complete electronic circuit, all of whose components are collected, or integrated on a single piece of semiconductor material, usually silicon.

interference The interaction between two similar waveforms. It generally results in either an increased or reduced amplitude of vibration.

ion An atom that has lost or gained one or more electrons. Metals lose electrons to form positive ions, or cations; non-metals gain electrons to form negative ions, or anions.

ionic bonding A form of chemical bonding that involves the transfer of electrons between combining atoms. Substances formed in this way are called ionic compounds.

kinetic energy Energy due to motion. Contrast **potential energy.**

kinetic theory The modern theory of matter, based on the idea that it is made up of particles (atoms or molecules), whose kinetic energy increases with temperature.

laser A device that produces an intense beam of parallel light of a single wavelength. The name stands for light amplification by the stimulated emission of radiation, which describes how laser light is produced.

lens A piece of glass or other transparent material with at least one curved surface. Lenses in optical instruments focus light rays.

liquid One of the three main states of matter, whose particles can move, but not independently. Contrast **solid** and **gas.**

magnetism A property possessed by iron and a few other metals of being able to attract similar materials. It is closely related to electricity.

mass A measure of the amount of matter in a body. Contrast **weight.**

matter The stuff of which the Universe is made up.

metallic bonding The type of chemical bonding that occurs in metals. Most metals have a crystalline structure in which their atoms are packed closely together. They contribute their outer electrons to a common pool. The presence of these free electrons helps explain why metals are such good conductors.

momentum The product of the mass and the velocity of a body.

motor, electric A device that uses electrical energy to produce mechanical motion. It works on the principles of electromagnetism.

Ohm's law When electricity flows in a conductor, the voltage is proportional to the current.

potential energy The energy stored in a body because of its position. A ball resting on a table has potential energy.

pressure The force acting on a unit area of surface, measured in such units as newtons per square metre.

radiation Energy given off in the form of electromagnetic rays or atomic particles.

reflection The bouncing back of waves (such as light and sound) from a surface.

refraction The bending of light rays that occurs when they pass from one medium into another.

resistance In general the property of a substance to oppose motion, as in air resistance. Electrical resistance in a conductor opposes the flow of electric current.

semiconductor A material that has properties between an electrical conductor and an insulator. Conduction is brought about by the presence of minute quantities of impurities. Silicon is the most widely used semiconductor. It is used in very small-scale integrated circuits.

spectrum The spread of colour obtained when light is split up into its constituent wavelengths.

static electricity The electric charge that builds up on some materials when they are rubbed.

superconductor An electrical conductor that has lost all its resistance. Some metals and alloys become superconducting at very low temperatures, within a few degrees of absolute zero. Others do so at higher temperatures.

transformer An electrical device that transforms, or alters the voltage of an alternating current supply.

transistor An electronic device made of semiconductor material that is used in electronic circuits for such purposes as amplifying (strengthening) signals.

vector A quantity having both magnitude and direction. Acceleration and velocity are vectors.

velocity The speed of a body in a certain direction.

voltage A measure of the potential difference, or electrical "pressure" in a circuit.

wavelength The distance between two successive crests or troughs of a wave motion (such as sound or light). For a given family of waves, such as electromagnetic waves, wavelength times frequency equals velocity. In the case of electromagnetic waves, this is the velocity of light.

weight The force experienced by a body due to gravity. In science weight is the product of mass and the acceleration due to gravity, and is measured in newtons. In everyday life, however, weight is usually expressed in mass units, such as kilograms or tonnes.

Index

Page numbers in *italics* refer to pictures.

A

acceleration 38, 43
alternating current 22
aluminium 14
amber 8
ammonium chloride 11
Ampère, André Marie 10
anode 10, 11, *13*
Antarctica 17
argon *13*
atoms 7
Australia *40*

B

barcodes 32
battery 10
   dry 11
   invention of 10
body scanner 20
boron 14
bubble chamber 7

C

camera 26
Canadian Arctic 17
capacitors *8*
carbon brushes 22
cathode 10, 11, *13*
cell 10
   dry 11, 14
centrifugal force 37
centripetal force 37, *37*
charges, electric 7, 8
chlorine 13
cobalt 17
coherent light 33
colour 30-31
commutator 22, *22*
compass 17
computer chip 14
concave lens 26, *27*
convex lens 26, *27*
copper 10, 20
copper sulphate 10

D

Daniell cell *10*
direct current 22, *22*

discharge tube 13
domains, magnetic 18

E

eels, electric 6
Einstein, Albert 24
electrical circuit *10*
electrical resistance *11*
electric bell *21*
electric charge 7
electric field 7, *7*
electricity 6-15
   measures of 10
   origin of 7
   static 8
   uses of *6*, 12-13
electrolysis 13
electrolyte 13
electromagnet 16
   in motors 23
   uses of 20
electromagnetic spectrum 34-35
electromagnetic waves 34, *35*
electromagnetism 20
electronic flashgun *8*
electrons 6, 7
   in generators 22
   in lasers 33
   movement of 10-11, *10*
   in semiconductors 14
electron waves 6
electroplating *13*
energy 40
   chemical 40
   conservation of 40
   electrical 40
   kinetic 40
   potential 40
   solar *40*

F

fibre optics *35*
filament 12
flashgun, electronic *8*
Fleming's rules 23
fluorescent light *13*
force 37
   electrical and magnetic 37
   of gravity 37
   strong 37
   weak 37
Franklin, Benjamin 8
Fresnel lens 27
friction 37, 39
fuse 11

G

Galileo 43
gamma rays 34
gamma-ray therapy *34*
generator 22-23
   principles of *22*
Gilbert, William 16
gold *15*
gravitational lens *42*
gravity 36, *36*, 42-43
   discovery of 42
   effects of 42
   on the Moon 42

H

hair *8*
heating 12
Hertz, Heinrich 35
Hipparcos 11
hologram 32
   production of 32
Hubble Space Telescope 26
hurricane 36
Huygens, Christiaan 28
hydroelectric power station *41*
hydrogen 13

I

images 26
   real 26, *26*
   virtual 26, *26*
integrated circuit 14
interference 28
iron 19, 20

J

jet aircraft *36*
Joule, James Prescott 40, 41
Jupiter 16, 43

K

kinetic energy 40, *41*

L

laser 24, 32-33
   invention of 32
   uses of 32, *33*
laws of motion 36, 38

lens 26
light 24-36
   coherent 33
   colours of 30
   disco *30*
   mixing *30*
   motion of 24
   speed of 24
   theories of 28
   waves 28
lighthouse 27
lighting 12, *12*
lightning 6, 8, *9*, 36
lines of force *18*
loudspeaker 12, 20

M

magnetic domains 18
magnetic field 18, 19, 23
magnetic force *17*
magnetic poles 17
magnetic variation 17
magnetism 16-21
   Earth's 16, 17, *17*
   and electricity 19
magnets, making of 18
magnifying glass *27*
Maiman, Theodore H. 32
manganese dioxide 11
Maxwell, James Clerk 34, 35
mercury *13*
microwave 35
   radar aerial *35*
migration 16
mining 23
mirrors 25
   curved 26
momentum 39
Moon 24
motion, laws of 38
motor 22-23
   AC *23*
   DC *23*
   function of 22
   principle of 23
   universal 23

N

National Magnet Laboratory 16
navigation 17
neon *13*
neutral point *18*
Newton, Isaac 26, 28, 36, 42
nickel 17
North Pole 17

nuclear fusion 16
nuclear magnetic resonance 20

O

Oersted, Hans Christian 19
Ohm, Georg Simon 11
Ohm's law 11
orbital 33

P

Panavia Tornado *36*
particle accelerator 20
photons 24, 29
poles, magnetic 17
positrons 7
potential difference 10
principal focus 26, *27*
prism 24
proton 7

Q

quasar *42*

R

radio, CB *35*
radio, short-wave *35*
radio signals 20
radio waves 34
rainbow *31*
   primary *31*
   secondary 31
reflection 25, *25*
refraction 24, 25, *25*
resistance 11
resistor 11
ruby (in lasers) 33

S

semiconductors 14, *14*
   doping of 14
   n-type 14
   p-type 14
silicon 14
snooker *39*
sodium chloride 13
sodium hydroxide 13
solar energy *40*
solenoid 19, *19*
sound 12

sound-to-light 30
South Pole 17
space satellite 11, 26
space shuttle 38
spectacles 26
spectrum 24
   electromagnetic 34
Sturgeon, William 20
sulphuric acid 10
superconductors 20

T

telephone 20
telescope 26
   reflecting 26
television 20
terminal velocity 43
thermograph 35
transformer *21*
tungsten 10

U

ultraviolet bed *34*
ultraviolet rays *13*, 34
universal motor 23

V

velocity, terminal 43
violet light 30
virtual image 26, *26*
Volta, Alessandro 10

W

white light 30, *31*

X

X-ray *34*

Y

Young, Thomas 28
yttrium-aluminium-garnet crystals *33*

Z

zinc 11

Further Reading

Take Nobody's Word For It by George Auckland and Bill Coates (BBC, 1989)
Exploring Magnets by Ed Catherall (Wayland, 1989)
The Young Scientist Book of Electricity by P. Chapman (Usborne, 1976)
Science Fun by M. Johnson (Usborne, 1981)
Moving Things (Science Alive series) by Robin Kerrod (Macdonald, 1987)
Focus on Electricity by Mark Lambert (Wayland, 1988)
Fun with Science by Brenda Walpole (Kingfisher, 1988)

Picture Credits

b = bottom, t = top, c = centre, l = left, r = right.
ESA European Space Agency. OSF Oxford Scientific Films, Long Hanborough, Oxford. RHPL Robert Harding Picture Library, London. SCL Spectrum Colour Library, London. SPL Science Photo Library, London.

4 SPL/Jan Hinsch. 6 Vautier de Nanxe. 7 SPL/Lawrence Berkeley Laboratory. 8l SPL/John Howard. 8r Minolta. 9 Zefa/T Ives. 10 SPL/David Taylor. 11 ESA. 12b Tim Woodcock. 12t Susan Griggs Agency. 13 RHPL. 14l Art Directors. 14r OSF/Manfred Kage. 15 SPL/David Parker. 16 SPL/U.S. Department of Energy. 17 SPL/Vaughan Fleming. 20l SPL/Alex Bartel. 20r SPL/Pacific Press Service. 21 Zefa. 23 Hutchison Library/R Aberman. 24 SPL/David Parker. 25 Robin Kerrod. 26 Perkin Elmer. 27l John Watney. 27r Robin Kerrod. 28l Paul Brierley. 28r SPL/Martin Dohrn. 29t ACE Photo Agency/Jerome Yeats. 29b SPL/Jeremy Burgess. 30 Zefa/K L Benser. 31 SPL/Phil Jude. 32 SPL/Hank Morgan. 23l Hughes Research Lab, Malibu. 33r SPL/Alex Tsiaras. 34t SPl/N M Tweedie. 34c SPL. 34bl SPL/Martin Dohrn. 34br SCL. 35t Institute of Electrical Engineers. 35ct SPL/David Parker. 35cr SCL. 35bl SPL. 35br SPL/Martin Dohrn. 36 Jerry Young. 37 RHPL/A Carr. 38t FSP. 38b SCL. 40 SPL/Andrew Clarke. 41t Zefa. 41c Hutchison Library/R House. 41bl Bridgeman Art Library. 41bc David Redfern/Stephen Morley. 41br Zefa/F Damm. 42 Spachcharts/NASA. 43t ACE Photo Agency. 43b National Maritime Museum.